Just**liv** ™

8 simple steps to living life with clarity and meaning

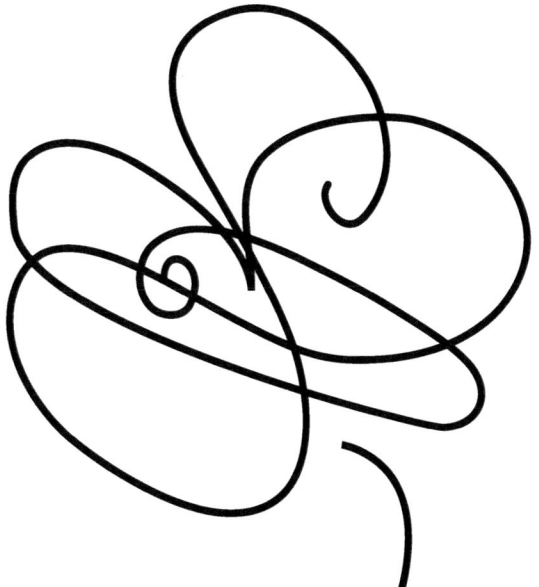

ISBN 978-0-9813986-5-5

LIV Publishing
Copyright © 2021 - 1187341 Sean LIV Productions Inc. - All rights reserved

ISBN 978-0-9813986-5-5

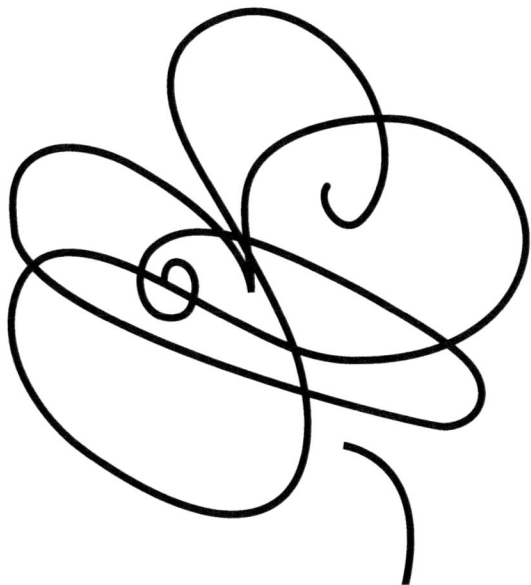

Dedication

To my daughter Hannah,,

my one truest love

Just **liv** ™

Life is a gift in itself. However, with society as it is, we collectively have created a place of fear, stress, competition and greed. But it doesn't have to be.

"Life is meant to be enriched with possibilities, with creative endeavors and emotional connections."

The following eight steps are a simple guide to help you release the burdens of your past, and let yourself be free from the pressures and illusions humans have stamped on our consciousness.

My hope is to allow you to experience the freedom to what life can truly offer you.

Be presence, be power, and be love.

xo

Sean

BECOME
THE
PRESENT,
not the past, or
the future

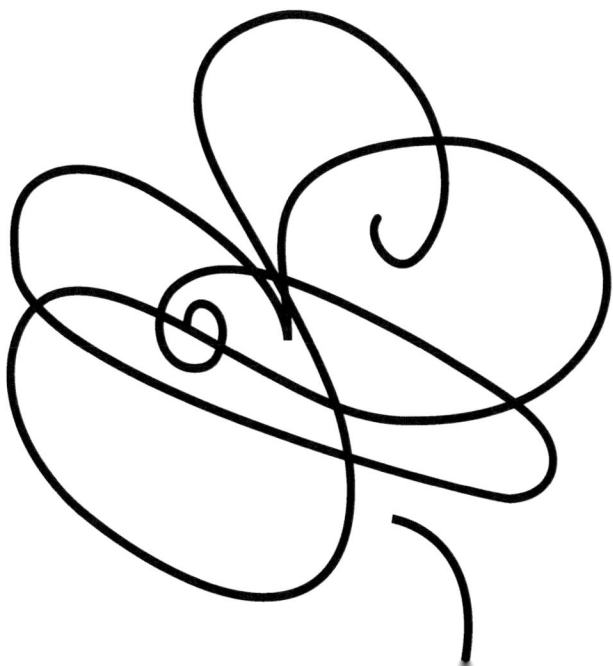

BECOME THE PRESENT,
not the past, or the future

The only moment you will ever really get to experience is right now.

We live too much with the burdens of the past, our to-do lists and the pressures of our society.

Life is too short not to live each day as it comes. It's truly a gift to yourself to understand this concept. Wasting time on worries or racing to the future or holding onto past regrets serves no purpose.

True power and joy come from being the best you can be in this moment for this day. Learning to liv daily - witness, feel and embrace each day - is a priceless gift. You will be able to set yourself free knowing that you can choose how you will write and plan your future.

liv

THERE's NO RIGHT or WRONG, or passes or fails in life

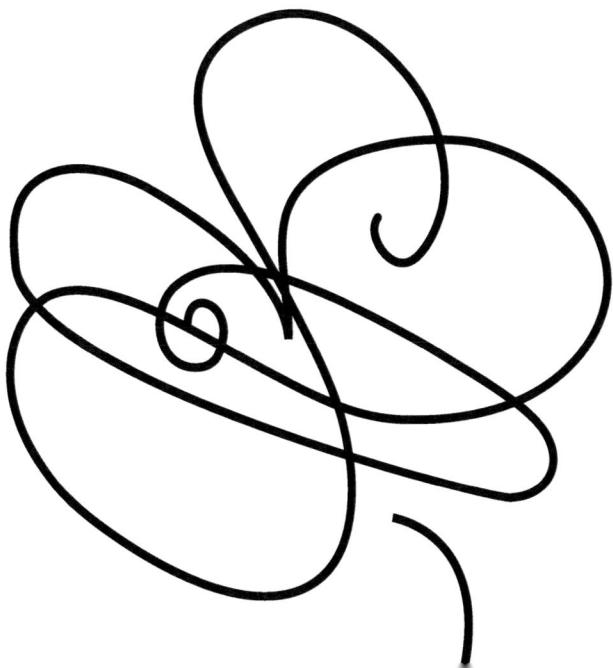

Step 02

THERE's **NO RIGHT** or **WRONG,** or passes or fails in life

It is all about the journey and the experiences, not the possessions or the status.

Remember this and know that wherever you are right now is where you are meant to be.

The regrets, the shame and the guilt of the "should haves" only hold you back from the true power that you have within. Relax knowing you have done the best you could until now.

● ●

liv

LIVE YOUR
LIFE
to the
FULLEST

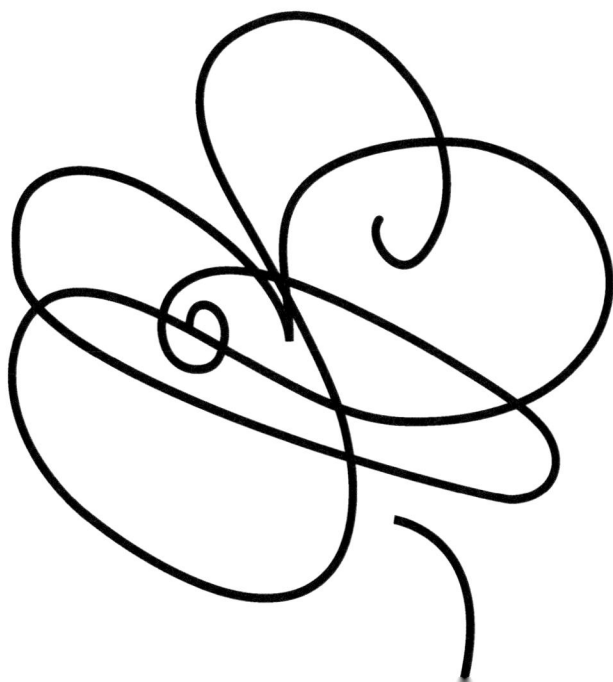

LIVE YOUR LIFE
to the FULLEST

Go and see the beauty of the world around you. There are many beautiful creations here on the planet.

They are to be experienced, not seen on TV or magazines.

Our world is the most amazing thing we have. This planet is magnificent. Witness the vastness of the oceans and the depths of our forests.

Climb a mountain.

Experience Mother Earth.

• • •

liv

CREATE YOUR REALITY

Envision your life as you want it to be

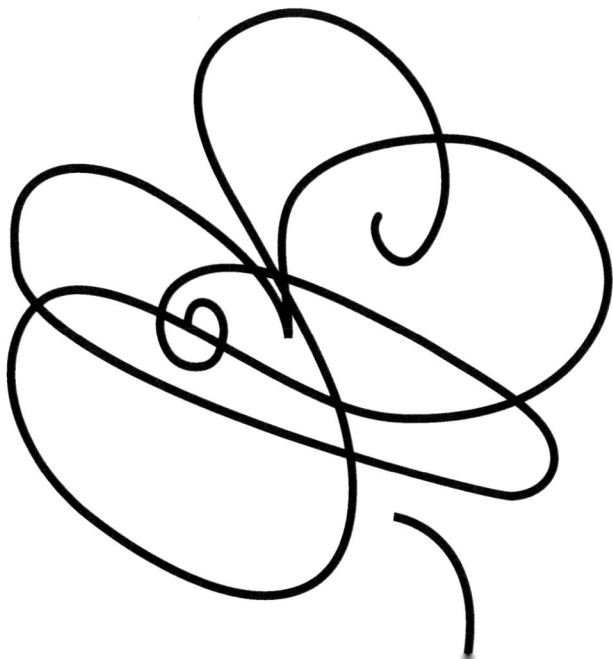

Step 04

CREATE YOUR REALITY
Envision your life as you want
it to be

It is fine to have the cars, trucks and SUVs but remember at the root of life is the heart. Lead your desired life through the eyes of your heart.

We need to consciously create the life that we deserve. What energy pathway do you choose to create?

Take time away from your busy life and sit with yourself and discover what it is your heart truly desires. You can have and create anything here in this life. If you have a dream or a passion, give yourself permission to go after it.

● ● ● ●

liv

Step 05

FORGIVENESS IS THE KEY

to anyone's life of fulfillment

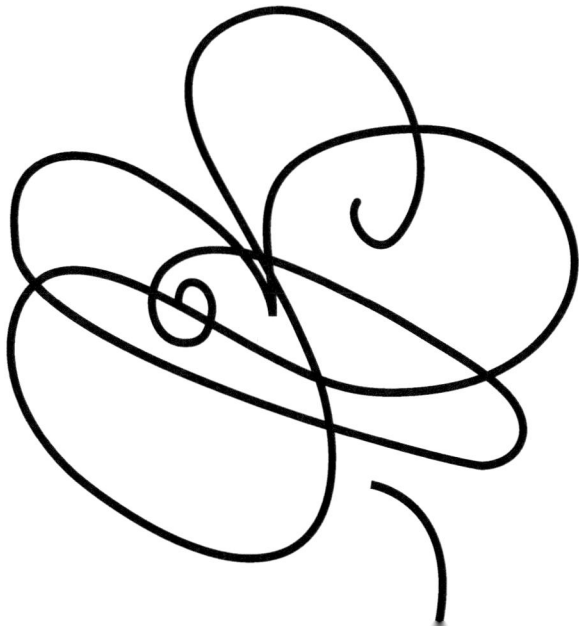

Step 05

FORGIVENESS IS THE KEY to anyone's life of fulfillment

If you can forgive yourself and combat the illusion of letting yourself down, that is the most powerful gift you can give to yourself

Forgiveness is granted to those who seek it. There is no step-by-step action plan for forgiveness, but if you choose to release the past and forgive what you perceive as mistakes, then you shall find freedom in yourself.

We're human and the more you love the good, the bad, and the ugly, the more beauty and self-love you will attain.

● ● ● ● ●

liv

●●●●●●

TIME IS AN ILLUSION
Take away deadlines and goals

Step 06

TIME IS AN ILLUSION
Take away deadlines or goals

Be open and allow yourself to be shown the way. Please do not plan, just go. Listen to your heart and allow this to be your guidance, your compass in life.

If it feels right, then do it. Remember you will know when you are prepared and ready to fulfill your purpose. Listen, and be guided in your truth.

As a society we are pressured into doing things by a certain time, and we carry on in this vicious cycle of accomplishments. When you're ready, you're ready. You can't rush the process. We can't rush a flower to bloom, we can't rush a child to walk. It all happens on its own time. Allow your life to unfold as you release your boundaries and flow into your presence.

● ● ● ● ● ●

liv

It's great to HAVE INTENSIONS but they should be filled with trust and faith

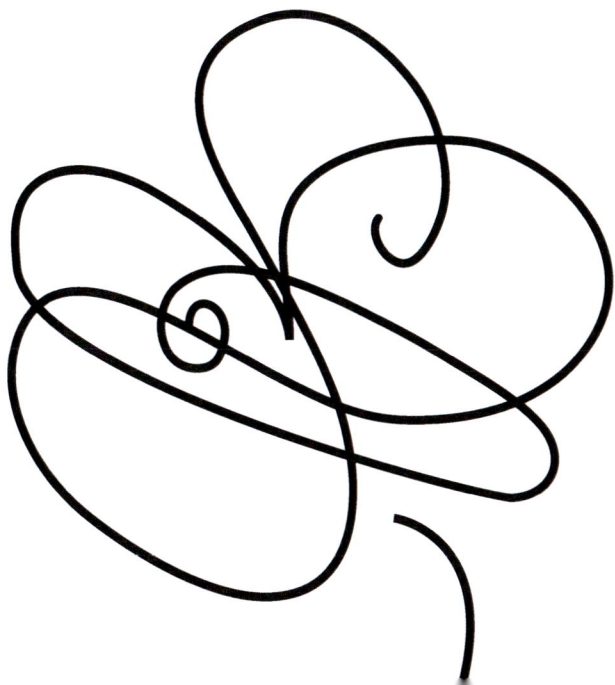

IT's GREAT to HAVE INTENSIONS
but they should be filled with trust and faith

Be aware of the energy spent on not so glorious things.

To truly become the magnificent soul you are, it's imperative that you listen and place your energy where it can grow. If there is no space for action then the creation process will die.

We all have dreams and desires to attain, however sometimes our minds and our lives are filled with so much noise that there is no space to grow. Time is on your side, but it's what you choose to do with time that will pay dividends in the seeds you have planted. A garden will not grow without the dedication of nurturing the seeds. Believe in your dreams and watch your possibilities grow.

● ● ● ● ● ● ●

liv

Be in a state of
PEACE &
Calmness. Realize there
is no final destination.

Be in a state of **PEACE &**
Calmness. Realize there is no final destination

The journey never stops. Remember there are always things to do and places to see.

but doing it without heart will only bring dissatisfaction. Peace is a state of the soul.

Close your eyes, and become this.

In our busy and plugged-in society, it may feel quite overwhelming. But peace is an inward journey. There is no person, place or item that can bring tranquility to you. It's a place where fear is set aside, anger and resentment are washed away, and we begin to feel the deep presence which is our birthright. This will lead you to living your truth as you deserve.

● ● ● ● ● ● ● ●

liv

About the Author

Sean Liv is the visionary program curator, coach, mentor, and teacher of Azuridge's Flourish - The LIV Well Spa. With her signature upbeat personality, energetic outlook, compassionate ear, and expertise in a multitude of health, wellness and spiritual techniques, she uplifts and inspires people every day.

After deciding to overhaul all areas of her life and set a new path, Sean built her career as a Transformational Coach, inspiring speaker, author of The Ticket, and founder of The Ticket to Change, a transformational program for the mind, body, and spirit. She is also the host of the award winning Liv Daily Show, an upbeat health and wellness show. She's passionate about helping people find the deep motivation that makes them unstoppable in connecting with their dreams.

Sean Liv encourages others to build a lifestyle that focuses on positive body, mind, and spiritual routines. Her own transformation journey gave her the tools to help people find life, inspiration and vitality.

FLOURISH
THE LIV WELL SPA AT AZURIDGE

www.ingramcontent.com/pod-product-compliance
Lightning Source LLC
Chambersburg PA
CBRC090825100426
42813CB00025B/2995/J

9 780981 398655